Bach Transcriptions for Organ

SELECTED AND ARRANGED
BY MARTIN SETCHELL

MUSIC DEPARTMENT

OXFORD
UNIVERSITY PRESS

OXFORD
UNIVERSITY PRESS

Great Clarendon Street, Oxford OX2 6DP,
United Kingdom

Oxford University Press is a department of the University of Oxford.
It furthers the University's objective of excellence in research, scholarship,
and education by publishing worldwide. Oxford is a registered trade mark of
Oxford University Press in the UK and in certain other countries

© Oxford University Press 2014

Martin Setchell has asserted his right under the Copyright, Designs
and Patents Act, 1988, to be identified as the selector and arranger of these works

First published 2014

ISBN 978–0–19–339902–0

Music origination by
Enigma Music Production Services, Amersham, Bucks.

Printed in Great Britain on acid-free paper by
Halstan & Co. Ltd, Amersham, Bucks.

CONTENTS

INTRODUCTION

Organ transcriptions of some of Bach's music, such as '*Jesu, Joy of Man's Desiring*' from Cantata 147, or the '*Air on the G string*' from the Orchestral Suite No. 3 in D, have long been part of the organist's standard repertoire. But there are many more such movements in Bach's huge vocal and instrumental oeuvre which make equally effective organ solos. This volume brings together a selection of my personal favourites from the cantatas, oratorios, Passions, and instrumental works. It includes a range of pieces suitable for service and recital use, and music appropriate for weddings, funerals, Christmas, and Passiontide.

I have refrained from too much editorial intrusion, especially in registration, allowing organists to make their own choices according to the instrument available. Tempo, dynamic, and ornamentation markings are original except for those in square brackets. Trills and ornaments should usually begin with the upper note on the beat. Any phrasing or articulation marked is original; suggested phrase breaks are shown by a comma placed above the stave.

It is my hope that these new transcriptions will help expand the Bach repertoire available to both church and concert organists. I am grateful to my editors at OUP, David Blackwell and Sean Bui, for their helpful comments and ever-vigilant eyes in the preparation of these pieces.

NOTES ON THE PIECES

Cantata movements

The festive **March** in D major was originally part of Cantata 207, written for an academic celebration in 1726. Eight years later, in 1734, Bach re-used this same music with a different text in Cantata 207a, for the name day of Augustus III, king of Poland and elector of Saxony. As befits its title, *Auf, schmetternde Töne der muntern Trompeten* (Blare forth, ye merry trumpets), the music was scored for three trumpets, timpani, violins doubling flutes and oboes, viola, and continuo. I have arranged it for solo Trumpet (ideally on a separate Choir or Solo manual) alternating with tutti repeats on the Great, with Swell coupled.

The serene **Sonatina from Cantata 106**, *Gottes Zeit ist die allerbeste Zeit* (God's time is best), is the prelude to a contemplative funeral cantata. The original scoring was appropriately muted, with repeated chords for two violas da gamba and continuo, supporting a 'sighing' melody played by two flutes à bec (recorders). Given Bach's obvious intention to reduce brightness by omitting violins and violas, stops with too brilliant a sound or excessively bright overtones should be avoided.

In a similar mood of quiet resignation is the opening **Sinfonia from Cantata 156**, *Ich steh' mit einem Fuß im Grabe* (I stand with one foot in the grave), written for the third Sunday after Epiphany, 23 January 1729. As the title suggests, Picander's text deals with preparation for death. This Sinfonia movement is a less richly ornamented version of the slow movement of Bach's Harpsichord Concerto No. 5 in F minor, BWV 1056 (itself derived from a lost violin or oboe concerto). My transcription combines both versions into one complete piece. Bars (measures) 1–20 comprise the complete Sinfonia from the Cantata (originally solo oboe, strings and continuo); bars 21–38 use most of the concerto slow movement (originally solo harpsichord, strings and continuo) transposed from A♭ to F major, with a final, long tonic chord at bar 39 in place of the original last three bars. If a shorter version is preferred, a cut may be made from the third beat of bar 7 to the third beat of bar 27, or by using the first section only, and substituting bar 39 for bars 19–20. The expressive melody needs a smooth, flowing legato throughout; if the Oboe stop is at all uneven in speech, it would be better to substitute another quiet solo reed stop.

Given the obvious string figuration of the right hand, it is no surprise that the **Sinfonia from Cantata 29**, *Wir danken dir, Gott* (We thank you, God), was originally the first movement (Preludio) of Partita No. 3 in E major, BWV 1006, for unaccompanied violin. When a new cantata was needed for the Town Council election in August 1731, Bach enlarged his exhilarating violin original, re-scoring it for three trumpets, timpani, two oboes doubling violins, viola, obbligato organ (right hand taking the original violin line), and continuo, and transposed it into the festive key of D major, which is more suited to trumpets. He also revived it in an unnumbered wedding cantata. Bach marked this movement 'Presto', but it must be remembered that his organ part was for manuals only on two staves. For this organ transcription I have suggested a more moderate Allegro.

Rinkart's famous hymn *Nun danket alle Gott* (**Now thank we all our God**), with its familiar tune by Crüger, has remained one of the strongest assertions of Lutheran faith. This version appears, appropriately, as the third movement of the Reformation Festival Cantata 79, *Gott, der Herr, ist Sonn' und Schild* (God, the Lord, is sun and shield), probably written in 1735. In the original, the continuous fanfare motif (also used in the cantata's opening movement) is scored for horns and timpani, with the periodic chorale phrases in full four-part harmony for chorus, reinforced by strings, flutes, and oboes.

My transcription aims to achieve a similar bold statement with the fanfare figuration as an organ pleno minus reeds in the right hand, and the chorale melody as a left-hand cantus firmus in the tenor on a solo Trumpet (or en chamade reed if available).

Movements from the large-scale choral works

There can be few more intense expressions of grief than the great final chorus of the *St Matthew Passion*, BWV 244: **Wir setzen uns mit Tränen nieder** (In tears of grief, dear Lord, we leave Thee). This organ version contracts Bach's original 128 bars to 80 bars, maintaining the movement's ternary (ABA) structure, but omitting the passages in the A section where the orchestra's statement is simply repeated by double choir. The sorrowful 'sighing' effects in the paired quavers, such as in bar 3, should be emphasized in the right-hand phrasing. The terraced dynamic markings (rare in Bach's music), and the echo effects between the two choirs (e.g. bars 8–10) are here replicated by manual changes. If a third manual is not available for the *poco piano* sections marked 'Choir', the effect should be conveyed on the Swell by further closing the box. At the end of the B section (bars 49–56), Bach's *piano* (bar 51) and *poco piano* (bar 53) clearly imply a *decrescendo*, so bars 51–6 should all be played on the Swell.

The **Pastoral Symphony**, which opens Part II of the *Christmas Oratorio*, BWV 248, sets the scene for the Evangelist's recitative which follows: 'Und es waren Hirten in derselben Gegend' (And there were, in the same country, shepherds abiding in the fields). Its rocking 12/8 rhythm, derived from the Italian *siciliano*, was a well-established musical image for the rocking cradle (cf. similar movements in Corelli's *Christmas Concerto* and Handel's *Messiah*). Bach's scoring alternates between a trio sonata texture (2 flutes doubled by 2 violins, and continuo), e.g. bars 1–9, and chordal versions with the contrasting timbre of four oboes da caccia, e.g. bars 9–14. If three manuals are available, the passages marked 'Sw. or Ch.' beginning at bar 9 could be played on the third manual. Bach also groups all the two- and three-note figures in one bow for the continuo bass instruments. I have shown this in the crotchet to quaver two-note figures only (e.g. bar 1), as it is not always practical for the feet in the three-note figures beginning with dotted quaver (e.g. bar 5); however, the legato should be observed whenever possible.

Instrumental movements

The trio texture of the **Largo** from the Concerto for Two Violins, BWV 1043, is very similar to the slow movements of the organ trio sonatas. Occasional bigger leaps (e.g. right-hand bars 26–7 and 30, left-hand bars 24, 29, and 39–40) and the typical cello line with its octave leap figures, point to the scoring for two violins and continuo. I have left the violin lines unaltered, but 'smoothed out' the cello line by replacing some octave leaps with repeated notes to avoid the 16′ pedal tone protruding, especially in lower-lying manual parts; it may be that Bach's *poco piano* marking in bar 1 of the continuo part was to warn against this potential bass imbalance in the concerto. A quiet and clearly voiced 16′ Pedal stop is crucial; if it is unavailable in the Pedals, and cannot be coupled down from an unused third manual, a clear 8′ bass line may be preferable. The carefully marked violin *détaché* quavers (e.g. bar 16, beat 2) should be clearly articulated.

The **Sarabande** was the usual slow movement of the four dances which formed the core of the Baroque Suite (Allemande, Courante, Sarabande, and Gigue). The dignified pace and restrained character of this ancient Spanish dance make it the most suitable for organ transcription. The two Sarabandes in this collection, from BWV 807 and 812, are both rich in expressive dissonances, which should be emphasised by a slow tempo and intense legato.

Dance suites in minor keys, with all movements in the tonic, were often provided with relief through one lighter movement in the tonic major; the G major **Gavotte** (**Musette**), BWV 808, and the A major **Bourrée II**, BWV 807, originally provided this lightness and tonal contrast. Both need a strong pulse of two, not four. The Musette's drone bass (pedal G) imitates the bagpipes, and is much more effectively sustained on the organ (preferably with a clear 8′ Pedal stop uncoupled) than the harpsichord.

Finally, I have included three pieces from Bach's repertoire for solo flute. In the familiar **Badinerie**, the playful dance which ends the Orchestral Suite No. 2 in B minor, BWV 1067, I have reduced the activity of the accompanying string parts to facilitate the lighter texture and fast tempo required. In the G minor **Siciliano** from the Sonata for Flute and Continuo in E♭ major, BWV 1031, the left-hand part is Bach's continuo right-hand line, except for bars 21–2 where I have transposed it down the octave to smooth the join back into the repeat of bar 1. In the **Menuetto I** from the Sonata for Flute and Continuo in C major, BWV 1033, I have maintained the spirit rather than the letter of Bach's realization, creating a lower part which avoids constant overlapping with the solo line. Bach left the A minor **Menuetto II** accompaniment as a figured bass stave only, so the left-hand chords are my own realization.

MARTIN SETCHELL
Christchurch, New Zealand, 2013

March

from Cantata 207a, 'Auf, schmetternde Töne der muntern Trompeten' (Blare forth, ye merry trumpets), BWV 207a

J. S. BACH
arr. Martin Setchell

[Maestoso]
Solo Trumpet 8'

Sw. (or Ch.)

16', 8' coupled

Printed in Great Britain

OXFORD UNIVERSITY PRESS, MUSIC DEPARTMENT, GREAT CLARENDON STREET, OXFORD OX2 6DP

Sarabande

from *French Suite No. 1 in D minor*, BWV 812

J. S. BACH
arr. Martin Setchell

Largo

from *Concerto for Two Violins in D minor*, BWV 1043

J. S. BACH
arr. Martin Setchell

Bourrée II

from *English Suite No. 2 in A minor*, BWV 807

J. S. BACH
arr. Martin Setchell

[poco rit. *2nd time only*]

Wir setzen uns mit Tränen nieder

(In tears of grief, dear Lord, we leave Thee)

from *St Matthew Passion*, BWV 244

J. S. BACH
arr. Martin Setchell

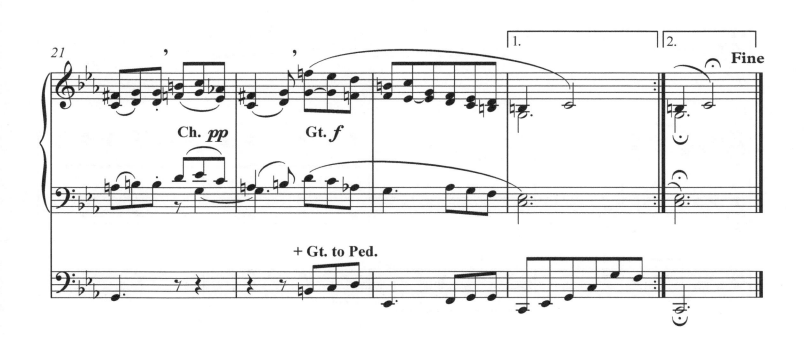

Badinerie

from *Orchestral Suite No. 2 in B minor, BWV 1067*

J. S. BACH
arr. Martin Setchell

Molto allegro e staccato

Sonatina

from Funeral Cantata, 'Gottes Zeit ist die allerbeste Zeit'
(God's time is best), BWV 106

J. S. BACH
arr. Martin Setchell

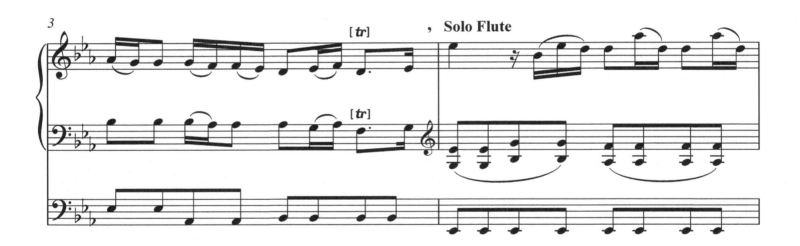

The original key signature for this piece has two flats with A♭ appearing as an accidental throughout. This cantata is also known as 'Actus Tragicus'.

Menuetto I and II

from *Sonata for Flute and Continuo in C major*, BWV 1033

J. S. BACH
arr. Martin Setchell

Menuetto I

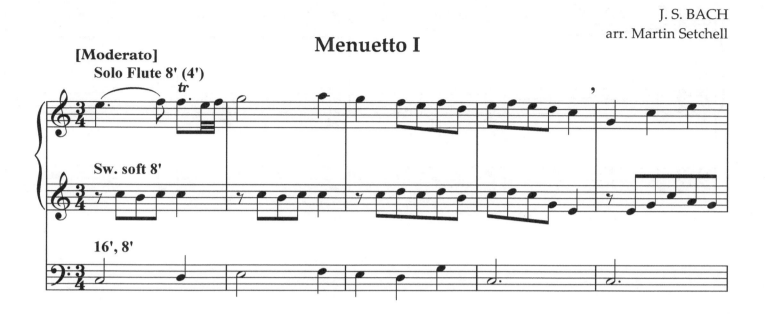

Menuetto II

Menuetto I Da Capo

Pastoral Symphony

from *Christmas Oratorio*, Part II, BWV 248

J. S. BACH
arr. Martin Setchell

Sinfonia

from Cantata 156, 'Ich steh' mit einem Fuß im Grabe'
(I stand with one foot in the grave), BWV 156

J. S. BACH
arr. Martin Setchell

[poco rall.]

Siciliano

from *Sonata for Flute and Continuo in E♭ major*, BWV 1031

J. S. BACH
arr. Martin Setchell

Gavotte (Musette)

from *English Suite No. 3 in G minor*, BWV 808

J. S. BACH
arr. Martin Setchell

Sinfonia

from Cantata 29, 'Wir danken dir, Gott'
(We thank you, God), BWV 29

J. S. BACH
arr. Martin Setchell

54

Sarabande

from *English Suite No. 2 in A minor*, BWV 807

J. S. BACH
arr. Martin Setchell

Now thank we all our God

from Cantata 79, 'Gott, der Herr, ist Sonn' und Schild'
(God the Lord is sun and shield), BWV 79

J. S. BACH
arr Martin Setchell